THIS BOOK BELONGS TO:

_____

WELCOME TO IOWA

Dedicated to all the explorers.

All rights reserved.
No part of this book may be reproduced in any form or by any means, electronic or mechanical, and no photocopying or recording, unless you have written permission from the author.

ISBN 978-1-958985-37-3

Text copyright © 2025 by Mimi Jones

www.joeysavestheday.com

A Mimi Book

IOWA

Iowa's name comes from the Iowa River, named after the Native American Ioway tribe. The name likely means "sleepy ones" in the Dakota Sioux language. Iowa became a U.S. territory in 1838 and a state in 1846.

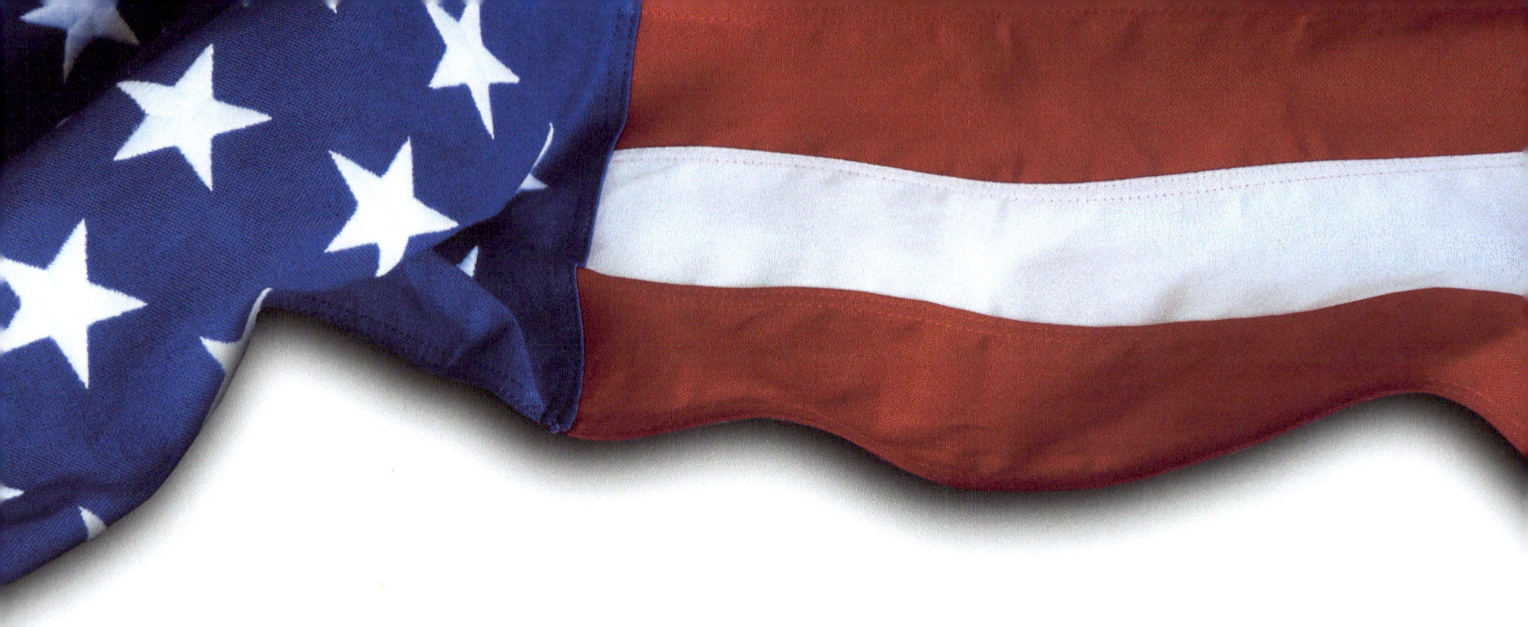

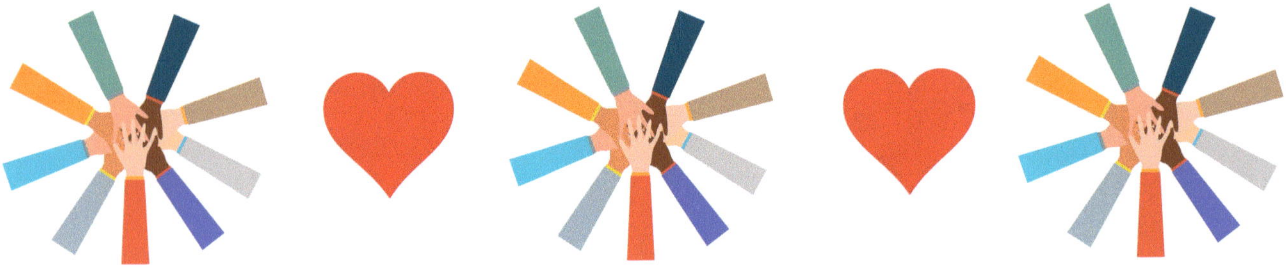

Iowa was the 29th state to join the Union.
It officially joined on December 28, 1846.

Iowa is located in the Midwestern region of the United States and is bordered by six (6) states: Minnesota, Wisconsin, Illinois, Missouri, Nebraska, and South Dakota.

Des Moines, a city located in the state of Iowa, officially became the capital in 1857.

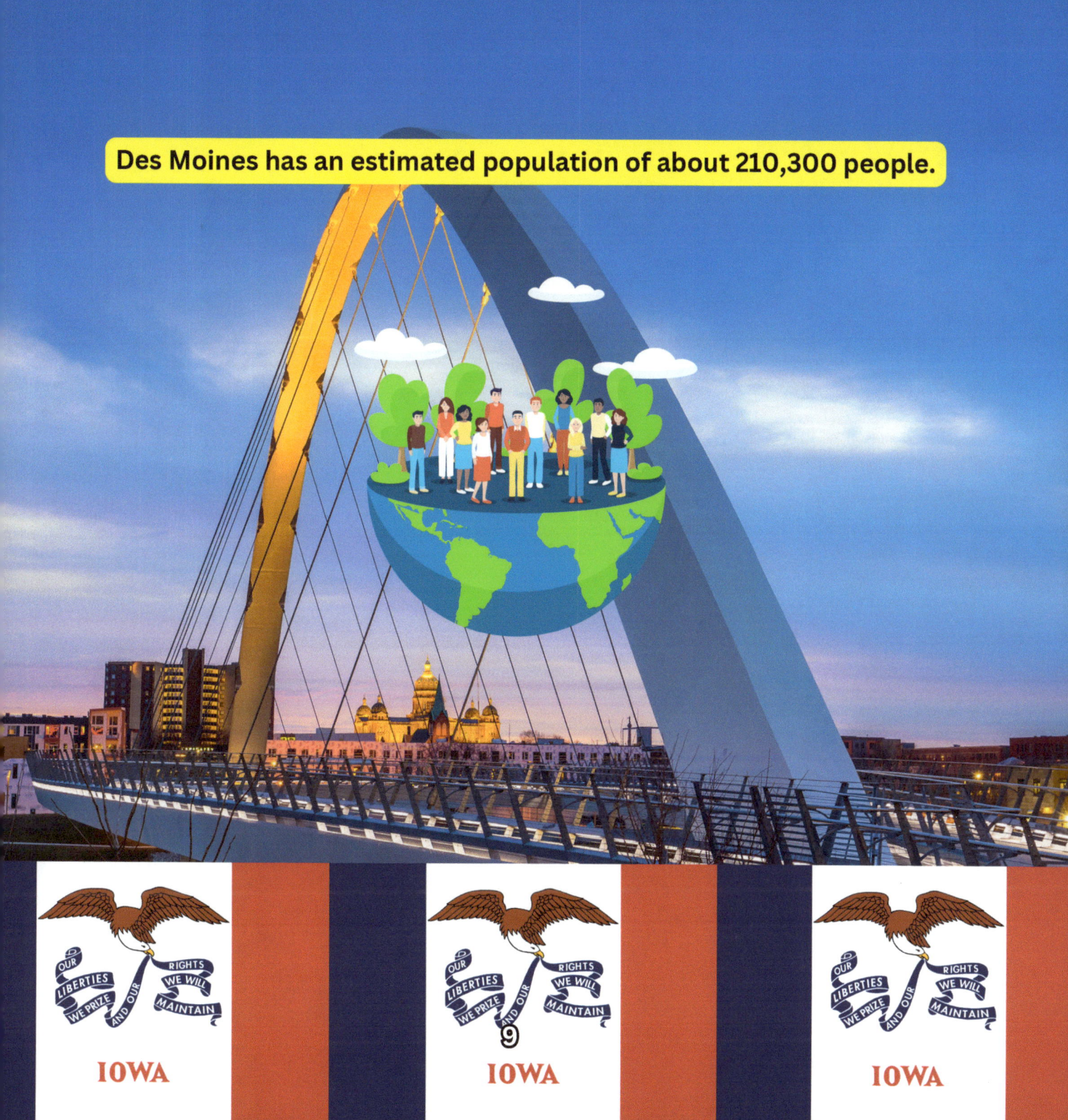
Des Moines has an estimated population of about 210,300 people.

Iowa, ranks as the 26th largest state in the United States.

Iowa State Capital
1007 E Grand Ave
Des Moines, IA 50319

There are about 3,207,000 people who live in the state of Iowa.

Waterloo, Iowa

George Nissen, born in Blairstown, Iowa, invented the modern trampoline in 1934 with coach Larry Griswold, inspired by trapeze safety nets. This invention transformed gymnastics and acrobatics.

Burr Oak Tree

In 1876, Laura Ingalls Wilder's family relocated to Burr Oak, Iowa, where they ran the Masters Hotel. Laura assisted with chores and lived in the basement. By 1878, they moved back to Minnesota, carrying with them memories of their Iowa experience.

Laura Ingalls Wilder, born in 1867, is famous for her "Little House on the Prairie" book series, which chronicles her family's pioneer life in the late 19th-century Midwest. Beginning with "Little House in the Big Woods," the series highlights the Ingalls family's adventures and challenges.

The Ingalls family resided in Burr Oak, Iowa, from 1876 to 1877. This chapter of their lives is depicted in Laura Ingalls Wilder's book, "Little House: The Long Winter." Today, the Laura Ingalls Wilder Park & Museum in Burr Oak provides a fascinating insight into their experiences during that era.

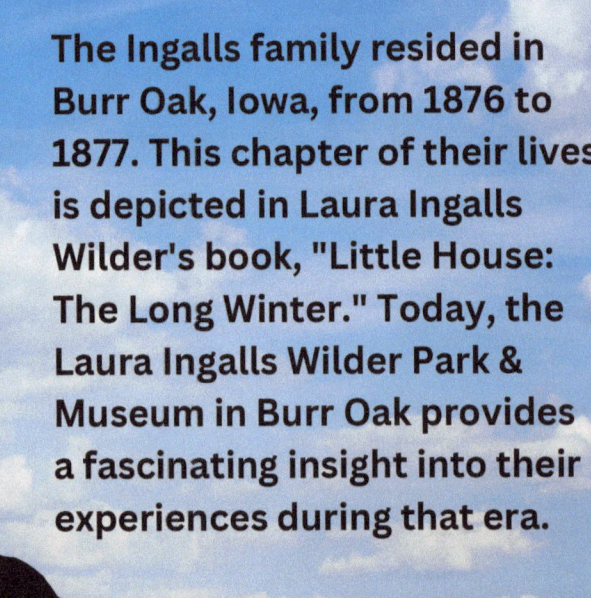

There are 99 counties in Iowa.

Iowa

Here is a list of 20 of those counties:

Adams	Dallas	Henry	Mills
Benton	Emmet	Ida	Page
Butler	Floyd	Jackson	Sioux
Cedar	Greene	Jasper	Union
Clay	Hardin	Louisa	Warren

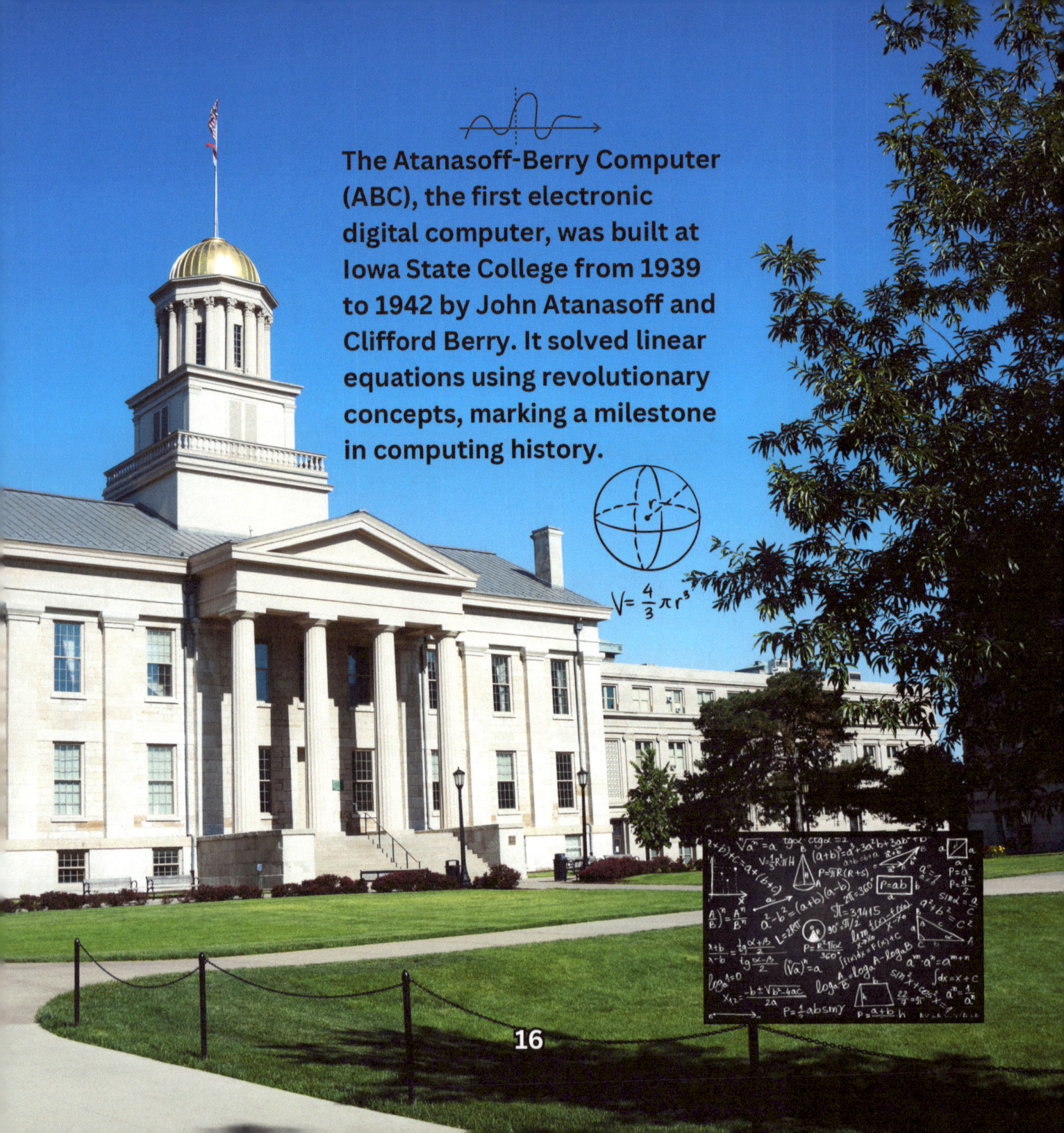

The Atanasoff-Berry Computer (ABC), the first electronic digital computer, was built at Iowa State College from 1939 to 1942 by John Atanasoff and Clifford Berry. It solved linear equations using revolutionary concepts, marking a milestone in computing history.

Grant Wood painted "American Gothic" in Eldon, Iowa, inspired by a Gothic-style house there. He used his sister and their family dentist as models.

Treehouse Village at the Iowa Arboretum & Gardens in Madrid, Iowa, opened in 2024.

Clark Tower in Winterset City Park, Iowa, is a 25-foot tall limestone structure built in 1926 to honor early settlers Caleb and Ruth Clark. It is a cherished local landmark.

Roller Coaster Road, located near Harpers Ferry in Allamakee County, Iowa, features a series of rolling hills that create a thrilling, coaster-like driving experience. It's a popular scenic drive, especially in the fall when the leaves change color.

Always follow the posted speed limits.

The Prairie rose was designated as Iowa's official state flower in 1897. It grows in various places throughout the state.

In 1933, the American Goldfinch was picked as the state bird of Iowa.

22

Iowa has several nicknames, including the Hawkeye State and the Corn State.

The Iowa state flag, which is currently in use, became the official flag on March 29, 1921.

Some crops grown in Iowa are corn, hay, oats, turnips, and wheat.

Some animals that live in Iowa are, bats, bobcats, deer mice, river otters, and white-tailed deer.

Iowa experiences extreme temperatures. The highest recorded was 118 degrees Fahrenheit in the city of Keokuk on July 20, 1934, and the lowest was -47 degrees Fahrenheit in Elkader on February 3, 1996.

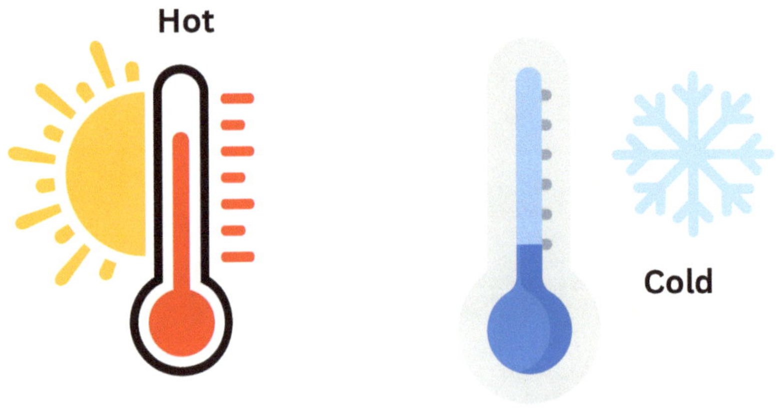

Hot

Cold

The High Trestle Trail Bridge is an impressive landmark situated in central Iowa, nestled between the towns of Madrid and Woodward. Spanning nearly half a mile in length and standing 130 feet high, this bridge is a key feature of the High Trestle Trail. It offers breathtaking views of the Des Moines River Valley and is known for its unique design, which includes illuminated blue lights and steel frames symbolizing the area's mining history. This iconic bridge is a must-visit for anyone exploring the region.

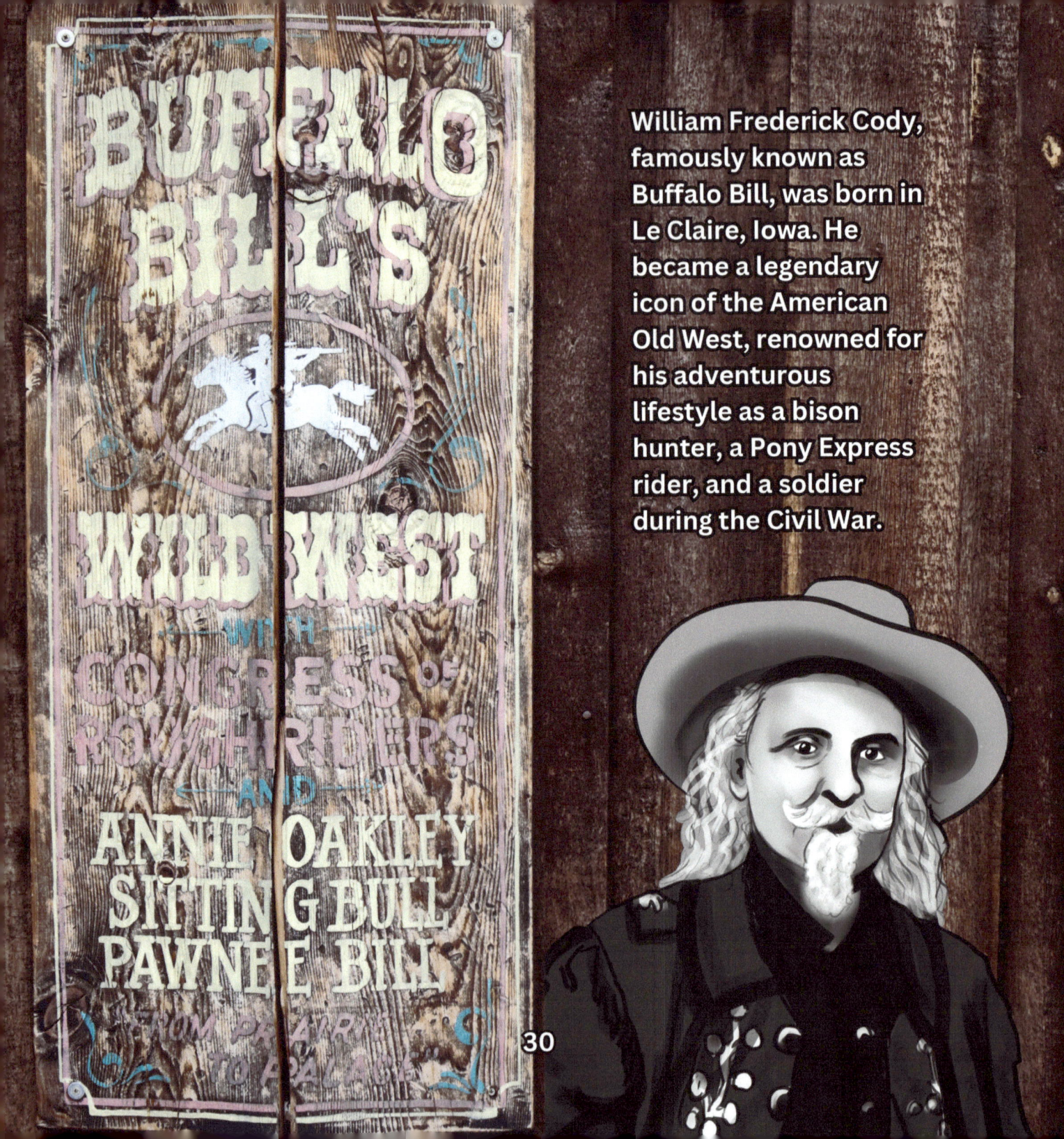

William Frederick Cody, famously known as Buffalo Bill, was born in Le Claire, Iowa. He became a legendary icon of the American Old West, renowned for his adventurous lifestyle as a bison hunter, a Pony Express rider, and a soldier during the Civil War.

Maquoketa Caves stands out as one of Iowa's most distinctive outdoor destinations. Majestic bluffs rise throughout the park, while a six-mile trail system meanders through stunning geological formations and lush forests, overflowing with natural beauty.

Maquoketa Caves
Maquoketa, IA 52060

  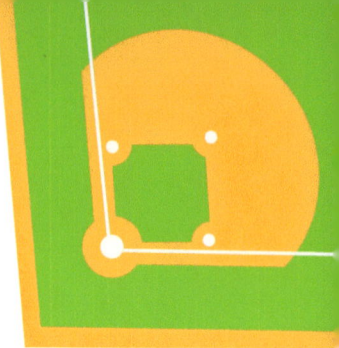

The Iowa Cubs, based in Des Moines, play in the Pacific Coast League. Other teams include the Cedar Rapids Kernels, Clinton LumberKings, and Quad City River Bandits. These minor league teams offer exciting baseball action and a more personal fan experience.

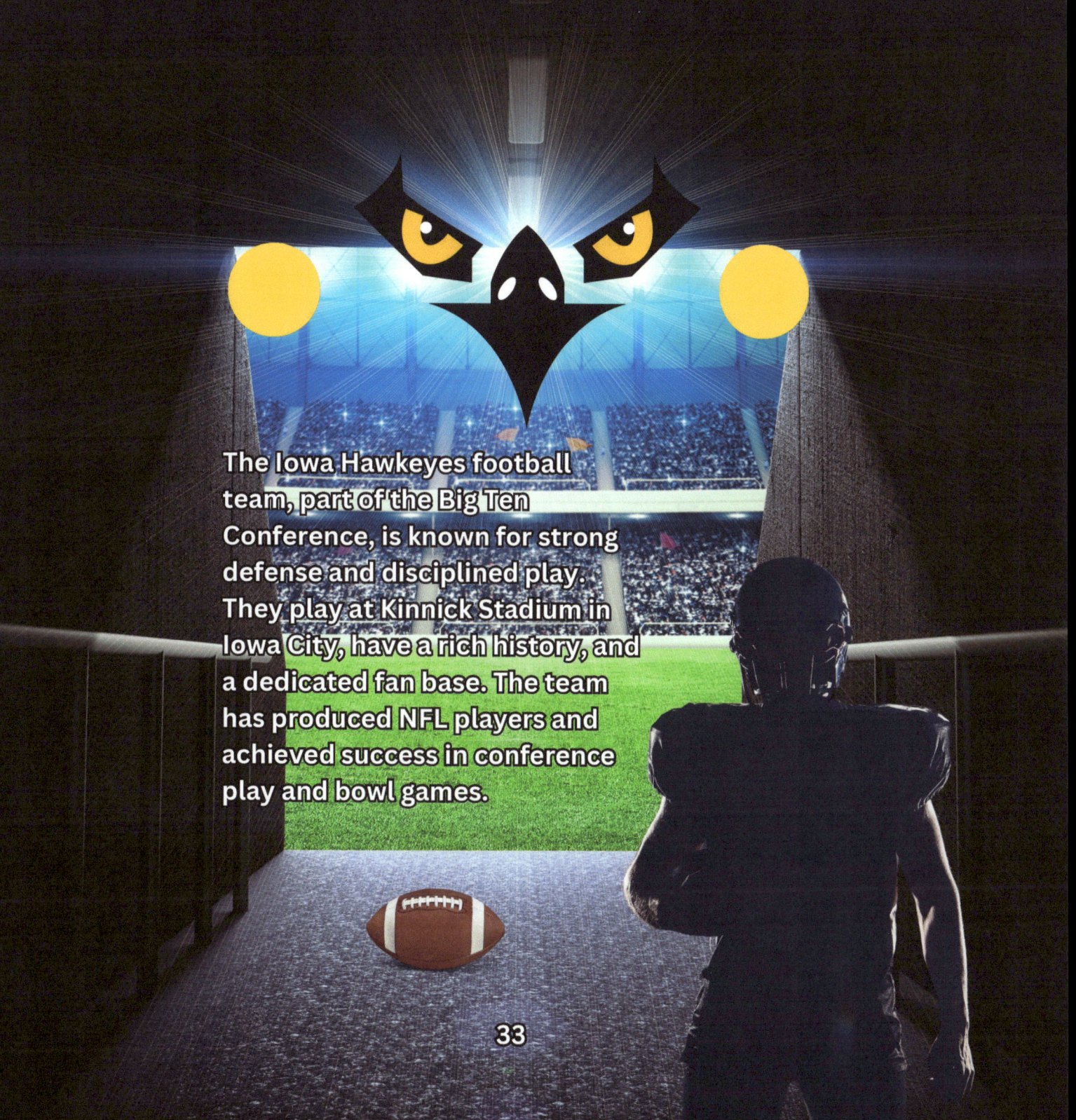

The Iowa Hawkeyes football team, part of the Big Ten Conference, is known for strong defense and disciplined play. They play at Kinnick Stadium in Iowa City, have a rich history, and a dedicated fan base. The team has produced NFL players and achieved success in conference play and bowl games.

Iowa is the only U.S. state with rivers marking both its eastern (the Mississippi) and western (the Missouri) borders.

River

Can you name these?

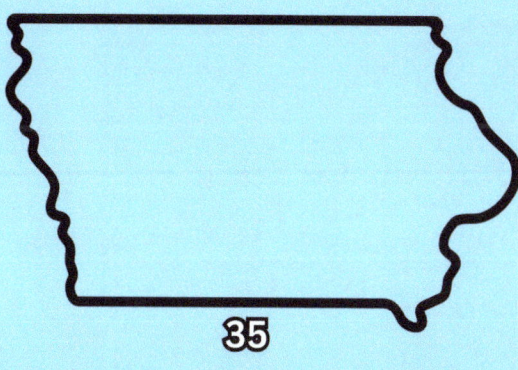

35

I hope you enjoyed
learning about
Iowa.

To explore fun facts about the other 49 states, visit my website at www.joeysavestheday.com. You'll also find a wide variety of homeschool resources to support joyful learning at home. If you enjoyed this book, I would be grateful if you left a review. Your feedback truly helps. Thank you for your support!

Check out these other interesting books in the 50 States Fact Books Series!

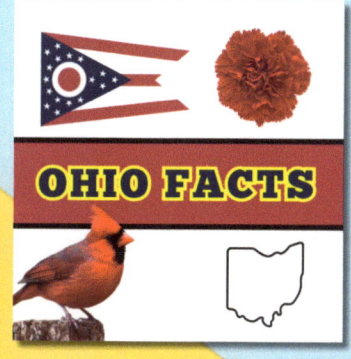

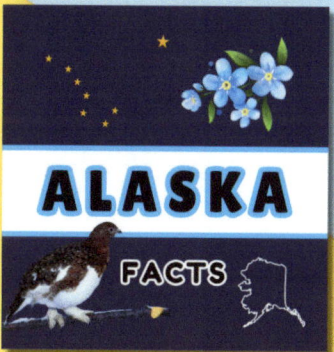

www.mimibooks.com